THE BOOK ON CLEANS

AND THEIR ROLE IN SPORTS PERFORMANCE

Chris Romano M.A., CSCS*D, RSCC, USAW-L2, FRCms, FMS

Table Of Contents

The Book on Cleans (and Their Role in Sports Performance)

Dedicated to my wife Christina, and children Lee, Alex, and Cali for all the time sacrifices they made for me to be the coach that I am.

I also want to dedicate this book to Coach Michael Cohen, who took me as a former baseball player and alpine ski racer and through his coaching and program, turned me into one of the top M35 weightlifters in the world. Thank you Coach; without you, this book would not have been possible.

Section 1

Intro:

Who is Coach Chris Romano and why am I qualified to write The Book on Cleans?

I have a master's degree in Strength & Conditioning / Exercise Science through LaGrange College, NSCA-CSCS with Distinction, NSCA-RSCC, USAW-Level 2, FRCms, FMS, ISSA Specialist in Strength &

Conditioning, Precision Nutrition Level 1, and OnBase University Pitching and Hitting certifications.

I primarily work with Baseball Players now, but have worked extensively with Football, Basketball, Lacrosse, Soccer, Softball, Rowing, Track & Field, Tennis, Cross Country, Competitive Cheerleading, and Cricket players. The primary focus of this book is going to be how and when cleans and their variations can and should be applied to the various sports, as well as how over the years, I have developed a very efficient and effective progression to safely teach the clean to athletes of the above listed sports. I have also competed at the top of the sport of Weightlifting, and understand how to take the tools and drills we use in that sport, and apply them to be effective exercises for sport athletes.

To make the most out of this book, I am breaking it down into three sections. Section 1 is on my background and common questions coaches, athletes, and the general public ask me regarding common myths and beliefs about weightlifting.

Section 2 is a very detailed explanation of how I teach new athletes the clean. It is a progression I have developed and tweaked over the past decade, and I see it almost as a bridge between what we did in the competitive weightlifting world and what is needed for the sports performance world. Knowing the audience of this book is primarily going to be sport performance / strength & conditioning coaches as well as sport athletes, I hope you find a lot of value in this progression, as I know it will include information new to most of the strength & conditioning community. Also, if you are reading this book, there is a good chance you follow me on social media, in particular twitter. Please feel free to reach out to me with specific questions and comments you have regarding the content in this book. I just remind you; this is how I teach the clean, and by no means is this the only way to do it. I am writing this book to help contribute to the wealth of knowledge the strength & conditioning community already has, and to hopefully help other coaches, as more veteran coaches helped me when I was younger.

Chapter 1

My Story: becoming a Coach

It was a warm summer's evening …. Just kidding, it was 1995 in suburban Atlanta so it was probably really humid and hot.

I first learned how to lift weights, including how to do a power clean back in 1995 during the summer before my freshman year of high school football at Walton High School. Even back then, I enjoyed the weight room more than practice or games. We were fortunate back then to have an actual "weight training" class at school. It was mostly the football players taking it back then, but it was a class that was available to all students, and to this day, I am still close with some of the kids from that class.

Fast forward now to 2003, as a senior in college, and coming off a knee injury and an elbow injury (I was a pitcher), I spent most of my time in the gym. My roommates and I went to a small gym in Central, SC because the Clemson Rec Center was always too crowded and we hated waiting on squat racks or machines (yes, I said machines; it was 2003 after all). It was there, in the upstairs of that small gym that I first noticed I really enjoyed training people, and teaching them how to lift properly. I had no formal training; I was an economics major at the time, but had learned how to lift in high school, and now was teaching my roommates how to lift as well. Others at the gym noticed and started asking for tips and advice as well, and while I didn't work at the gym, and probably shouldn't have done it, I was happy to help.

After graduating in 2003 with a B.S. in Economics, I moved back to Atlanta and was considering what career path I wanted to take. My elbow had not fully recovered from surgery, and despite getting one offer to play independent league baseball down in Louisiana, I decided to enter the real world and get a job. So, I went to the local LA Fitness and interviewed to be a personal trainer. They offered me the job, and gave me the materials to study to become certified.

Now, you're probably thinking this is when I first became a coach, but it was not to be. While I was studying for the personal training exam, through a college connection, I had an incredible job opportunity fall in my lap. It was using my economics background and traveling around the country for a financial services firm. I literally got to travel to all 50 states for meetings with financial advisors and stockbrokers. Being 23 years old, this was an opportunity that I couldn't pass up. I was able to set my own schedule, and being so passionate about baseball, I made sure to catch games at every ballpark. I also got to work out in many unique gyms. This job led to another job, which eventually landed me in Washington DC working for the entity that regulates the financial markets and mutual funds (I would need their permission to name them in the book so we'll leave it at that description). Since this job didn't involve travel, I became a regular at the local Gold's Gym. The job also paid VERY well. Being single, and still in my late 20s, it also allowed me to take ski trips all around the world. I took up ski racing as a hobby, and was doing very well with that. By 2010, I was skiing on the FIS Masters World Cup Circuit in the US, South America, and Europe. During one winter, I made 4 weekend trips to Europe, 5 to Colorado, and one week in September skiing in Chile. I ended up getting sponsors to help fund the racing, even though I was really just an average racer compared to the other competitors. One of the sponsors was Gold's Gym, the gym where I was a regular in suburban DC. The financial job paid very well, but I wasn't happy sitting in a cubicle all day with very little human interaction. I had a set amount of work that needed to be done each month, and as long as I hit that quota, the bosses were happy. So, I made sure to get most of the work done within the first week of the month (which I would plan as my recovery week), and then spent the majority of the rest of the month training. I'd spend an hour in the fitness center of the office building, then hit Gold's for a couple of hours after work. Some days I would go for an 8-10 mile run during my lunch break too. It was the definition of Over Training, but at the time, I didn't know any better. By 2012, I was more focused on my time in the gym than I was on actual skiing. It was then that I realized that if I was going to be really happy in life, I needed a change. My wife's job was in Atlanta, so moving back down there seemed like the smart move. It also meant an end to the skiing hobby, which ended up working out perfectly since our first son was born in 2013. I brought up the idea of leaving the financial sector to my wife, and proposed the idea that we open a gym. Being the cautious and financially conservative type, she said no to the idea of opening a gym, but said she would support the idea of me becoming a personal trainer. So, I joined a local gym, got certified to be a coach, took the USAW Level 1 Coaching Course, and became a part time group fitness trainer.

I coached at that gym for the next 3 years, becoming their head trainer and was in charge of their Olympic weightlifting program. We hosted multiple USAW coaching courses and various weightlifting workshops. I really fell in love with the cleans and snatches over this time.

Fast forward to 2016. I was finally at a point where Christina was comfortable with me owning my own gym, so we bought Atlanta Strength & Conditioning. It had a very small client base, but within the first three months, I was able to triple the membership. The gym was at a point where I could hire a staff to run most of the group fitness classes, and I could focus on growing the athlete centered side of the business. Over the 3 years of owning the gym, I was fortunate enough to have an MLS team use the gym while their training grounds were being built, had college baseball players, Olympic hopefuls, and Olympians all train with me there.

It was also during this time that I met Coach Michael Cohen. Of all the coaches with whom I have worked, he probably had the single greatest impact on me as a coach. For those that do not know him, he was a 1980 Olympian and Head Coach of the US Olympic Weightlifting Team in the 2000 and 2004 Olympics. Michael started training me as a competitive Olympic Weightlifter, and I really found my sport. With him, between 2016 and 2018 I competed at 3 Arnold Fitness Festivals, 3 Masters Pan Ams, and 2 World Championships, as well as several American Opens and 2 National Championships. I won the silver medal for individual total at the 2017 Pan Ams in Santiago, Dominican Republic, 2 silver medals at the 2018 Pan Ams in Gaspe, Quebec (individual total & team total), 6th place in the 2019 Pan Ams in Orlando, 22nd at the 2018 World Championship in Barcelona, and 9th at the 2019 World Championships in Montreal.

During this time, I also assisted Coach Cohen in teaching the USAW Level 1 Coach's Course, as well as assisted him in several different types of weightlifting clinics and seminars. I was fortunate enough to coach multiple National level weightlifters during this time as well. My reputation in Georgia started growing as an Olympic Weightlifting Coach, and in December of 2017, I was given an opportunity to go full circle and go back to Walton High School to work with the football team. Once a week during their weight training class I helped them with their clean technique.

Being back in a team setting, I very quickly realized what direction I really wanted to take my career. I hired more staff to cover my mid-day sessions at Atlanta Strength & Conditioning, and started volunteering every day with the football team. That led to the basketball coach asking me to work with his team, and eventually the baseball coach letting me work with his team. That all took place in the weight room that was located in the basement of our Fieldhouse. In 2020, we opened a new weight room that was located in the school and word spread that there was a qualified strength coach available. I soon had 9 sports teams bringing me in to work with their athletes. For the first time in the history of the school (dating back to 1975), we had an equal number of girls & boys teams weight training. The schedule eventually became very packed, so I started an internship program in 2020. The interns help manage large lifting sessions, but I am also able to teach them what I know. We cover sport science topics such as technology, energy systems, nutrition, and biomechanics. I also teach them the progressions I use for each lift, including my detailed clean progression, which we will cover later in this book.

As of the writing of this book, I have coached Olympic weightlifting on 3 continents in English, Spanish, Italian, and German settings. I have coached all levels of athletes. I have worked with 4 year olds, middle schoolers, and high schoolers. I have also worked with two collegiate programs, and interned in professional baseball.

Chapter 2

Myths surrounding the Olympic lifts, who can benefit from incorporating them, and when to use them

This chapter will address a lot of the common questions I hear regarding myths surrounding the Olympic lifts, as well as discuss appropriate scenarios of when to use the clean and the jerk, and why I do not program snatches for any of my sport athletes.

Q: When is an appropriate age to start teaching a child how to lift?

A: This is by far the most asked question I get, in particular every time I post a video of my son lifting on Twitter or Instagram. My answer is whenever that child shows he/she is physically and mentally able to handle a complex movement. Let me elaborate.

The child/athlete needs to be able to understand the verbal instructions you are giving, or be able to imitate what you are demonstrating (assuming you are demonstrating it well). I'll start by using my two sons as examples. Lee is the oldest, and Alex is the youngest. Lee was 2 when I was primarily training at home. I would sit him in his playpen where I could see him (and he could see me) while I lifted. By the time he was 3, he was imitating my clean and jerk and snatches with a PVC pipe, and doing a really good job, so I bought him a plastic set of toy weights from WodToys. He also came with me to most of my weightlifting meets, and in 2016 at the American Open in Miami, he expressed interest in going up on the platform. He kept doing well and seemed to really enjoy it, so when he was 4, I bought him a 2.5KG OSO barbell, which is made for children. His form was better than most adults by this point. I brought him with me to the 2018 Arnold Fitness Festival in Ohio, and we brought his OSO bar to the training hall. He did snatches on the platform next to me while I snatched, and did clean and jerks next to me while I did mine. Everyone in the training hall noticed this little kid slinging weight around. By the end of my training session, the director of USAW and a former Olympic Gold Medalist both came by to see him. Long story short, USAW ended up manually inputting his info into the membership system that wasn't capable of registering a 4 year old, so he could do a meet. 3 weeks later, in Savannah, Lee did his first weightlifting competition. By the time he was 6, he won state championships in the youngest age class in both Georgia and Tennessee. He has really taken off in Baseball, and with the throwing he does for that, I have taken snatches and jerks out of his training (I will go into a detailed explanation of the rationale behind that later in this chapter), but he still does cleans whenever he asks me. I make it a point to never ask or tell him to lift. He only does it when he wants to, and when I deem it a smart time, based on his baseball schedule. Even at his young age, training stress and volume is a key factor.

Now, Alex is the exact opposite case. He has expressed interest in lifting, but when he was 2-3 years old, I was not training at home, so he did not watch me every day. He does not have the coordination his older brother has to be able to take my queues and implement them. He is an excellent back squatter, but when I walk him through the clean motion, he isn't able to apply it yet. Therefore, when he asks to lift, I set him up in a squat rack. He squats 50% of his body weight (he is 41 Lbs). He could physically handle cleaning a 2.5kg barbell, but mentally he is not ready yet. Same family, but a different athlete, so a different program is necessary.

This brings me to the need to evaluate your athletes as soon as you begin working with them. Even at the high school level, there are certain athletes that are not yet capable of performing a clean correctly. Therefore, I have them do a menu of other movements to achieve the same set of adaptations we aim for with the clean.

Let me take this opportunity to address the elephant in the room regarding the topic of children and weights. Given the audience of this book, I do not feel the need to go into much detail here, but nonetheless, I want to cover all my bases. Over the past 21 years, there has been plenty of research (led by Avery Figenbaum) regarding resistance training in children. To summarize the findings of every one of these peer reviewed studies, it does NOT stunt growth. In fact, resistance training during growth spurts has been found to stimulate bone density, thus reducing chances of a broken bone later in life. Additionally, Olympic weightlifting for children develops coordination and confidence at a young age. If you disagree with this, please look at Dr. Figenbaum's research; it can be accessed free of charge on Google Scholar and PubMed.

Q: I have heard sports such as baseball, softball, and lacrosse should not do cleans. Is that correct?

A: In general, any athlete in a sport that requires power output would benefit from a clean. Now, I know where this myth comes from, and I sort of agree with it. Let me explain. If an athlete is unable to hold a bar in the front rack with proper form (elbows pointing directly ahead, humerus parallel to the floor), there will be a lot of stress on the elbow, in particular, stress on the UCL. In throwing sports, such as baseball, softball, and lacrosse, there is already a lot of stress on the UCL, so adding extra unnecessary stress on top of what is accumulated through the sport is unwise. There are plenty of other ways to develop power besides an Olympic lift; those ways are just much less efficient. So, assuming it is okay with the sport coach and training staff, AND you are competent in teaching the clean, I do not believe there is a single better way to develop power for an athlete who is capable of performing the lift with good technique. One key part to this last sentence is "if the sport coach and training staff are okay with it". As a sports performance coach or strength & conditioning coach, it is important to remember that in the high school and college settings, we are there to assist the sport coaching staff to help their athletes obtain the muscular and physiological adaptations needed to be at their best for their sport. If the sport coach does not want his team to do a particular lift, then other alternatives need to be made. In the professional sport setting, the goals are the same, but the decision to use certain lifts would come from the high performance coordinator as an organizational decision.

Q: If an athlete has a previous injury, for example, a shoulder dislocation that would limit their ability in the weight room, how would you incorporate weightlifting derivatives?

A: This question was asked to me by another coach, in relation to hockey players. I haven't worked with hockey, but I would address it the same way I would with any athlete with a joint stability issue.

The first thing I do in this situation is consult with our Sports Medicine team to determine if and when the athlete can start a CARs program. For those that are unfamiliar with CARs, it stands for Controlled Articular Rotation. It focuses on increasing the range of motion for the joint in question. Once the athlete demonstrates good ability to rotate the joint, I would then go back to our Sports Medicine staff to see if the athlete would be approved to begin a Pails and Rails program. Pails and Rails is Progressive Angular Isometric Loading and Regressive Angular Isometric Loading. It basically is a way to strengthen the stability of a joint without having to move said joint. Many times, an athlete recovering from injury can begin this before they can begin a regular training program, and it is an excellent way to help the athlete get stronger in the area where the injury occurred. I know this is new material to many of the coaches reading this book, so I would highly suggest spending some time researching CARs and Pails and Rails on Youtube to get an idea of what it is, and then, if it is something you see value in, I highly recommend the FRCms program through Functional Range Seminars.

In this specific example, aside from the CARs and Pails and Rails program to strengthen the injured area, we would still need to address the goal of increasing the athlete's power output. Depending on the location of the previously injured joint, you have a menu of alternative exercises to use.

If it is a lower limb injury, your most similar option to use would be a modified glute bridge. I've had several cases with ankle injuries where we can isolate the injured limb and get in some quality glute bridges or hip thrusts in. If it is a hip or spinal injury, you can't use that option.

Alternative options for upper body joint injuries are more plentiful. Let's use the dislocated shoulder example mentioned earlier. Power development is the intended stimulus, and power is defined by force times velocity. That athlete could benefit from doing medicine ball cleans, while focusing on the velocity side of the power equation. Then they could do some weighted jumps holding dumbbells at their side to focus a little on the force part of the power equation. Another alternative would be glute bridges, as mentioned above. If you have the technology, and the shoulders are stable enough to hold a bar, you could do some Velocity Based Training as well. This answer is now starting to trend toward the time efficiency topic, which will be addressed later in this book.

Q: When do you Jerk, and why don't you program Snatches?

I feel like this is a topic that I could write an entire book on, and it is probably the topic that started the idea for this book. Let me first address the question on jerks. The sports for which I would suggest incorporating jerks as a team would be sports where an athlete needs overhead power, such as basketball, lacrosse, competitive cheerleading, and volleyball. For sports such as football, I would only ask positions requiring overhead power and overhead strength to train jerks. For example, a wide receiver or defensive back would see a lot of benefit from training jerks, where as an offensive lineman or linebacker would see less benefit transfer over to the field from training jerks. One thing to note on jerks is first, before teaching the jerk, you need to be sure each athlete has the shoulder range of motion as well as shoulder stability to perform the jerk properly. If they cannot catch the bar over the center of their head due to lack of shoulder mobility, that needs to be addressed first. As discussed earlier, I would start them on a CARs program for this. In the event you have an athlete recovering from injury, but is able to safely hold weight overhead there are alternative movements to the barbell jerk. For example, I currently have two girls basketball players who lack the rotational ability in the shoulder to get the bar overhead, without pain. For those two ladies, we do dumbbell jerks with their hands internally rotated. They get a very similar stimulus, but pain free. Then we address the pain issue through CARs. Understanding the biomechanics involved in each lift allows you as a coach to be able to make adjustments in situations like this, instead of just saying "ok, you don't jerk, and you don't clean".

Now, the question of why I don't have my athletes snatch comes up quite a bit, especially since when I was a competitive weightlifter, the snatch was by far my favorite lift. This comes down to two reasons, the second being more important than the first. 1) The way our weight room is designed, I am not comfortable teaching our athletes how to bail on a snatch. We have 12 platforms, but each platform is in front of a squat rack. There are only two platforms that do not have a dumbbell rack directly in front of them. So basically, you only have the designated platform area to safely bail, with no room for error to "chase under a bar" or to bail forward and fall backwards. However, even if we had a different set up, I still would not have 99% of our athletes snatch, due to reason number 2.

2) Risk vs Reward. On this, I think back to a slide presented in the USAW Level 1 course (1). The peak power output of a 100Kg/220LB male on a clean is 5500 watts. This peak output would be seen in the second pull. The peak power output during the first

pull of the clean (just the liftoff portion) was stated at 2950 watts. The peak power output on the snatch was also 5500 watts, during the second pull. However, the peak power output of the first pull on the snatch (the liftoff) portion was slightly higher than that of the clean, at 3000 watts. In my professional opinion, when considering whether to program snatches or cleans, the extra shoulder mobility needed, the more complex lift, and catching the barbell overhead is not worth the additional 50 watts seen in the first pull. Therefore, I say the snatch does not justify the added risk.

Now, I say the extra risk, only as it relates to the clean. When examining injuries per 100 participants in high school sports, Olympic weightlifting has a 0.0035 injury rate as a whole, much lower than varsity high school sports (football 0.10, basketball 0.03, track & field 0.57, cross country 0.37)[2]

Q: Is there a particular warmup you have found to be more successful than others?

A: When training multiple teams, it is vital to be efficient. Having a consistent warmup when applicable really helps save time. On days we clean, all of my athletes know that when they come into the weight room, they go straight into a warmup. This allows me a little extra time to work with the previous team or group of athletes, or to talk with the sport coaches and our sports medicine staff.

I also have gotten into the habit of having certain sports start their session off with either CARs work or some reactive drills. After they do the initial individual work, they can then proceed over to the platforms and start the following barbell warmup. Please note, this is only for days we do cleans. Other days, we have specific warmups directed at the movements we will do on those days.

My warmup consists of 1 round without putting the bar down of:

5 Romanian Deadlifts

5 Shrugs

5 High Pulls from the Low Hang

5 Front Squats

5 Tall Cleans (explained in the definitions section)

5 Hang Cleans (explained in the definitions section)

Then they usually start with around 50% of their 1 rep max on the bar and do a few reps, then move up to 60% for a few reps, and then begin their working sets.

Now, I would like to take a minute here to explain that I do not address programming in this book, and that is for a very good reason. I firmly believe that programming needs to be athlete, team, and coach specific. For example, we both may be training high school football players, but our athletes may need different adaptations, our sport coaches may have different S&C goals, our schedule (days and time) with each athlete may be different, and our overall athlete work load/volumes may be very different. Therefore, my program may work very well for my team, but would not necessarily be appropriate or successful for your team. Without knowing specifics about the team and athletes, it is impossible to be confident in writing a successful training program. Thus, the goal of this book is to explain HOW I coach and teach the clean, and not how I apply it to my athletes and teams.

CHAPTER 3

To Pull or to Catch?

If you're reading this book, you fall into one of three categories. You're either a sports performance / strength & conditioning coach, you're an athlete looking for answers, or you're a friend of mine just reading the book to be nice. If you're in that first group, odds are you are on Strength Coach Twitter. Like clockwork, the argument between the "we catch" and the "we only pull" camps breaks out every few weeks. Inevitably, someone always tags me in the discussion assuming I am in the "catching" camp. Here's the thing though, currently I am. However, that is completely due to my current situation running a 3500 sq ft weight room, with 12 platforms that I can see all at the same time, working with athletes that I have coached since they were either in middle school or freshmen in high school, and a staff of interns to whom I have taught my clean progressions. If and when any of those factors change, my outlook might also change.

The answer whether to pull or to catch is going to basically come down to several follow up questions. 1) What stimuli does the athlete need based on their sport and their position(s) played? 2) How many weight room sessions does the athlete get each week? 3) How long is each weight room session? 4) Is the whole sports performance staff competent in teaching a clean?

Let's look at my first follow up question, "what stimuli does the athlete need?" If you're a head strength coach or head sports performance coach, whether you work with only one sport or multiple sports, I truly believe it is absolutely vital to know the biomechanics and bioenergetics of each position of each sport you train. Yes, I said it, and I do know that will touch more than a few nerves with several coaches in the high school universe. However, sports performance is a science, and if you're going to be very very good at what you do, it is something that needs to be understood. You cannot train an offensive linemen the same way you train a striker in soccer. Using that example, which of those athletes would really benefit from the catch portion of a clean, vs for which one would the catch not be as important? Clearly, the offensive linemen would benefit more from the catch, including the squat portion of the clean, while the striker would benefit from the catch, but perhaps not enough to justify the added training stress.

Now, let's take a look at the second and third follow up questions together, since they are interrelated. How much time do you have with each athlete, and how many days do you get them? For me, this varies per sport and per season. For example, our Football, Baseball, and Boys Basketball teams have weight training as a class, so they're in the weight room 5 days a week for 45 minutes a day (ignoring Covid-19 years), while on the other extreme, our girls lacrosse team comes in for an hour once a week. Most of the sports I work with at the high school come in two days a week, and most of the college and pro-weight rooms I have been in have athletes lifting 2-3 times a week. My point is, every situation is different, but those differences factor in my answer. I love cleans; if I didn't I wouldn't have written this book. I am fortunate that all of the sport coaches at Walton allow me the freedom to program as I see fit. Thus, each team I work with at the school does cleans. But, let's say that wasn't the case, because for the majority of the coaches reading this book, it likely is not the case. If you have a team that comes in 4-5 times a week, you have options. You don't necessarily need to worry as much about efficiency. If you want to use ten different exercises over the course of the five days to address force and velocity adaptations, you have that luxury, without having to really sacrifice another adaptation. However, let's say my girls lacrosse coach, for whatever reason, doesn't want her girls cleaning. Just on the weight room end of the sport, they need power production, rotational balance, lower body and upper body strength, as well as both anaerobic and aerobic training. I have 60 minutes every 7 days to address those goals. If I couldn't use a clean (full clean including squat), there is no way to get all of that even remotely covered. How do I manage it? Well, they warm up and then do cleans. Through cleans, they train power AND lower body strength. The pull portion gives them the velocity and force production, and the catch at the bottom gives them the concentric squat portion. Some weeks we do squats, but we don't have to, because they're getting that out of the clean as well. After the cleans, we can address the upper body strength, and I can manipulate rest periods, reps and sets to address the energy system needs. However, without the ability for them to do cleans, there would be no way to cover everything.

I will now address the 4th follow up question, which really only applies to large schools or professional teams. If you have multiple coaches working with athletes in the weight room, there needs to be consistency in both vocabulary and ability. If I am with the baseball team on the baseball field, and an assistant is in the weight room with the varsity competition cheer team, and the assistant cannot effectively teach the clean, then I lose the ability to program that movement. Therefore, if you are going to incorporate cleans, like any other movement, your staff needs to be competent to teach them. If they are not, then you are better off doing alternative exercises with your athletes until the entire staff that would be coaching is competent to do so.

SECTION 2

Teaching the Clean

Chapter 4

Let me start this section with the assumption that all athletes being taught this progression have been put through a movement screening (preferably FMS or OnBaseU type of objective screening). At a minimum, this gives the coach confidence the athlete will be able to put his/her body in the positions required for each of these steps. If at any point you find a mobility or injury situation that prevents proper technique, it needs to be addressed via your athletic trainer or through a mobility program such as CARs, which we previously discussed.

Step 1:

The Medicine Ball Clean

Ok, this step will be unlike any of the following steps, due to the fact it has multiple steps within itself. However, I have found most athletes are able to learn the medicine ball clean within one session, or at the most, within two sessions. I cannot think of a single case where an athlete has passed movement screening and not been able to advance past the medicine ball clean by the end of the second session.

MBC Step 1: I ask the athlete to simply pick the ball up, hold it at the hips, without bending their elbows. Then I say, "This is the top of the deadlift position." It is just easier to explain since most athletes know what a deadlift is – remember, the big art to coaching is being able to take complex concepts and make them simple enough for the athlete to understand what you want them to do.

MBC Step 1

MBC Step 2: I ask them to sit the ball on the floor and stand over the ball with it between their feet.

MBC Step 3: I put them in the proper set up position-hands on either side of the ball, shoulders over the ball, but chest up, back flat, and butt to the back wall. The primary difference between the MBC setup and the barbell setup is the hands are going to be internally rotated on the MBC.

MBC Step 3

MBC Step 4: I ask them to take the ball to the top of the deadlift position without bending their elbows, by pushing the floor away from them. From here we do several reps, so I can ensure their hip hinge pattern is good and they're maintaining form without bending their elbows.

MBC Step 4

MBC Step 5: I ask them to start from the top of the deadlift, and to squat under the ball, and help them get into the proper catch position. In this step, as they get the hang of it, we increase the speed at which they "drop" under the ball. I also explain this is similar to a hang clean, which we will do later with a barbell. I try to teach my athletes as much as possible, since an educated athlete is much easier to coach and work with than an uneducated athlete.

MBC Step 5

MBC Step 6: We combine everything, and they perform a Medicine Ball Clean from the floor. We work to not bend the elbows early and increase the speed with each repetition.

Medicine Ball Clean

There are a couple of coaching points that I would like to bring up here. We all know that if you can address a fault early on in an athlete's development, it will be much easier and faster to fix than if you allow something to slide for a while. With that said, over the past decade of working with athletes and general population clients, two of the three most common faults I see with a clean can be addressed very easily in this early stage.

The first fault that I am more than willing to take the time to address at this point of the progression is not getting full hip extension. Most of the time, this is caused by one of two issues. Either the athlete isn't used to having to fully extend the hips (more often this happens with general population clients who sit at a desk most of the day), or they want to bend their elbows early.

To address the first issue, depending on the experience of the athlete, I like to either use Kettlebell Swings, or hip thrusts/glute bridges. Once I see they can extend the hips, we go back to the MBC. If I observe they are still unable to extend the hips doing either of these exercises, we revert back to correctional exercises to address the issue.

It is much more difficult to address the issue of bending the elbows early. I know this first hand, because as an athlete, I was guilty of this for years. It wasn't until Coach Cohen queued me to finish the deadlift portion and then pull the bar as I drop under it, that I was able to make the correction. Therefore, this is an easier fault to correct with verbal queues, assuming the athlete reacts well to verbal queues. If you need to address it movement-wise, having them go through a tall clean is a way to correct an early elbow bend. Tall Cleans are defined in the definitions section in the 3rd section of this book.

Step 2: The Clean Finish

After completing the medicine ball clean, I bring the athlete(s) over to a squat rack to learn the Clean Finish. The bar sits on top of jerk boxes, or in a squat rack, or in the safety spotter straps/bars at a height where you can hold the bar at the position of the top of the first pull. You then squat under the bar, keeping your chest next to the bar as you descend. You shoot your elbows under the bar, now at the low point of your squat, while in the front rack position. Then you stand up. It is imperative to start with the bar in a rack or on boxes and NOT lift the bar off that platform until you stand up out of the bottom of the squat. Otherwise, you would be performing a Tall Clean, not a Clean Finish.

The Clean Finish

→ Bar does not
Leave RACK
Until

Step 3: The Set Up

Now that the athlete knows how to perform the most dangerous portion of the clean, we can then teach the next most dangerous portion of the lift. This is also the stage that either sets the athlete up for a successful lift or a failed attempt. In the Olympic lifts, there are so many complex moving parts that must be done near perfectly to have a successful lift. Thus, it is no surprise that a poor set up will doom the lift before the bar even leaves the floor. Inevitably, when teaching this progression, this is the stage where I end up spending the most time, and queuing the athlete the most. Now I will highlight key points to the setup, not in any particular order. They all must be completed before the bar leaves the floor!

Hand Width: I always start the athlete by having them measure their grip to be a thumb's distance from where the knurling meets the smooth part of the bar. In most cases, this will be slightly wider than shoulder distance, thus allowing for the athlete to transition into a proper catch position. It is also the ideal width grip when performing a conventional deadlift, and keeps the shoulders in a safe position. If their grip on the bar too narrow or too wide, they will not be able to have your elbows up in the front rack.

Grip: I have mixed feelings on the grip used when coaching sport athletes. The hook grip IS the most effective grip when doing a clean (or a snatch). The hook grip is when you grip the bar with your index and middle fingers on top of your thumb, with the thumb, ring finger, and pinkie in contact with the bar. This works best when using a quality barbell that spins. The hook grip allows the bar to spin as you transition past the second pull into the catch position. It is also a stronger grip and allows you to pull more weight off the floor, as opposed to a pure "death grip". If you are training competitive weightlifters, you likely aren't reading this book though, and in reality, a competitive weightlifter is the only one who needs to use every advantage to lift the most weight possible. As sport performance coaches using cleans, we are only concerned with our athletes' safety, and helping them get the intended stimulus, in this case, power development. Since we know the highest power output on a clean is between 65% and 75%, we do not need to use the hook grip to be able to pull an extra few pounds. Therefore, I teach it to everyone, but give them the option to use it or not. Now, if bar path becomes an issue due to not being able to rotate the elbows through fast enough using a death grip, we then revisit the hook grip. As a side note here, while discussing peak power output percentages, I generally only program weights between 65% and 80% on cleans for most of my sports. Football is the one exception where we go heavier to get the force absorption benefit of the catch under heavier loads.

Shins & Bar Placement: There is some variance allowed here. Ideally, the athlete would begin with the shins perpendicular to the floor and the barbell slightly touching the shins. However, that requires elite mobility on the athlete's part, and most sports you train outside of gymnasts/cheerleaders will not have an entire team capable of getting into this start position. In order to maintain proper back position, and to give the opportunity to have proper bar path, you can allow the knees to move forward during the setup as needed. However, it is important to remember that we are not starting from a squatting position; the first pull is essentially a hip hinge very much like a deadlift. If compensating by allowing the knees forward at the setup, you, as the coach, need to watch very closely in the next step to make sure the bar is traveling straight and close to the body, as opposed to getting away from the body.

Head/Eyes: Just like anything else, you want to maintain a neutral spine. I often see an athlete start with a bent neck, either looking up or looking down at the floor. The neck is part of the spine and therefore, it needs to be in alignment. I always prefer to have my eyes looking at something on the floor about 10-15 feet in front of me. That is just personal preference; I focus on that so I don't get distracted by movement (or in the case of 2019 World Championships in Montreal seeing my dad in a bright blue shirt in the front row of the upper level of the stands distracting me and making me miss my first two snatch attempts).

Slack: This is one step most coaches outside of the competitive weightlifting world seem to overlook. The plates and the barbell do not sit completely flush with one another. There is a very small gap between the inside ring of the plates and the barbell. If the athlete does not get that slack out of the bar before starting the first pull, there will be energy lost and a slight inefficiency in timing of the entire lift. I always instruct my athlete to slightly lift up on the bar, just enough to hear or feel the top of the bar meeting the bottom of the inside ring of the plate before they fire off. This also inadvertently engages the athlete's hamstrings, ensuring a good lift off/first pull.

- **Hands and elbows outside Knees**
- **Back and neck in neutral position, eyes looking 10-15 feet forward on the floor**
- **Bar against shins, 90 degrees to the floor**
- **Toes angled out slightly**

STEPS 4 & 5:

The 2ⁿᵈ Pull & The 1ˢᵗ Pull

Now we move on to a few of the easier steps to teach. Steps 4 and 5 usually move quickly and just take a matter of minutes for most athletes. Due to their similarity and quickness, I am grouping them together in this book.

I get the athlete in their setup position and ask them to deadlift the bar and hold at the top. From here, I ask them to push the ground away at the same time they high pull the bar using their upper back, arms, and shoulders (again, remember we keep it simple for the athlete). I also ask them to "keep the bar against your shirt the whole time."

Once they demonstrate the ability to do that well, I queue them to lower the bar at the start position from the hips to the knees, by driving their hips backwards. We then continue to high pull from that position.

After doing several of those repetitions, I then start them back in the setup position, and ask them to do the same thing we just did, but to do it from the floor. Now they are doing the 1st and 2nd Pulls. Key points are to ensure the bar path stays close to the body, elbows do not bend before reaching the end of the 1st pull, and to make sure they're fully extending the hips. If at any point they do not check off all those boxes, you should consider regressing or working on correcting the mobility issue.

StepS 6 & 7:

The High Hang & The Low Hang Clean

While these two steps take some athletes a long time to progress through, there is not a whole lot for me to write about them that we haven't already covered.

At Step 6, I ask the athlete to again take the bar to the top of the deadlift, and then combine the pull and the clean finish. Most of the time they are able to do that part fairly quickly. When I move on to step 7, things change a little. I ask them to start at the top of the deadlift, then to lower the bar to the knees by driving their hips backwards, and then quickly change direction and accelerate the bar upwards. The most common mistake made here, and for some reason the hardest habit to break, is pausing at the knees before changing directions. I have had some success by demonstrating the stretch shortening cycle using rubber bands or resistance bands, but even with the athlete knowing they should not pause, often they still do. It is the easiest fault to see as a newer coach, but one of the most difficult to overcome.

As a side note, I almost always program deadlifts using the hex bar. In my professional opinion, it puts the athlete in a safer position by not having the load in front of their center of mass. Over the years, most of the injuries I have personally witnessed in weight rooms and gyms have come from someone trying to lift more weight than they are capable. I have also noticed that of all the lifts, more people (in general), try to be a hero on a deadlift. I think a large factor is the load does not ever go above your body in a deadlift, so the fear of dropping the bar on yourself is not there. Therefore, this is a riskier situation than I would like in a room of 40-45 high school athletes, regardless of what they're instructed to do percentage-wise. Thus, to get the straight bar deadlift stimulus, I prefer to use a controlled method: The Hang Clean. By programming in the hang clean, the athlete has to do a full deadlift before cleaning the bar. However, the load will not be at a high percentage of their 1 rep max deadlift since they know they also have to clean the load after deadlifting it. Therefore, this is one way I can intentionally limit the risk of an athlete attempting more weight with a straight bar deadlift than desired. They can get the heavy load stimulus on a day we use the hex bar for deadlifts.

High Hang

Low Hang

* elbows are straight in both positions

1 Knees are unlocked/slightly bent in both positions

→ hamstrings are <u>not</u> loaded

Back is flat and upright

→ back flat but torso is at a slight angle

→ hamstrings are loaded

*elbows straight in both positions

*Knees bent/unlocked in both positions

*Hamstrings not loaded (in high hang position)

*Back is upright (in high hang position)

*Back is flat and angled (in low hang position)

*Hamstrings loaded (in low hang position)

STEP 8: The Clean

Now we put it all together. Before reaching this step, the athlete has demonstrated proficiency in each of the previous steps. Therefore, we know with 100% certainty they are physically able to hit all the positions involved in a clean, safely and efficiently. This is probably the easiest stage to coach, as well as the most fun, because you see the reaction the athlete has when they do a movement they believed to be complex and hard with relative ease.

The Clean

*Notice the bar is = height in the transition from the pull
to the catch. Speed under the bar is key!!!*

Chapter 5: Application

Now, I know a lot of strength coaches are wondering at this point why there was not a step to include the power clean. Simple, it is MUCH easier for an athlete to perform a power clean after learning a clean than the other way around. If I want to have the athlete perform a power clean, all I have to do is ask them to not catch the bar in a full squat. But teaching them to do the power variation first, and then asking them to squat under it is mentally much more difficult. Remember, they're sport athletes and probably don't understand why we ask them to do different variations of the clean, so in their eyes, asking them to now squat under it is asking them to do more work than they have to, when in fact, it is a different stimulus.

I have indirectly addressed when and how I apply cleans and their variations at points within this text. However, now I will address this topic directly.

For the teams I coach, I generally have them clean in the offseason, hang clean in the pre-season and non-region season, and do hang power cleans during the season or regional play and playoffs. My rational for this is the fact that the primary goals for the offseason are building strength and hypertrophy. For this reason, I want the athletes doing the squat portion of the lift. For collision sport athletes, I want them to also get the added benefit of absorbing the load in the catch position. As I stated earlier in the book, when we can address multiple goals with one movement, there is no need to use a menu of other movements. That just wastes the athletes' valuable time. During pre-season or non-region play at the high school level, the volume of sport time has increased, therefore requiring us to lower the volume of training stress. However, we still need to be efficient with our time, and we still see the benefit of including the squat portion for both training adaptations and time efficiency. But, by changing from the clean to the hang clean variation, we now eliminate the deadlift portion from all but the first rep of each set, thus saving some training stress. During the key portion of the season, which generally doesn't last more than a month for most of our sports, including 5 regional opponents, and state playoffs, as a sport performance coach I am happy to trade the strength benefit of an extra squat day, plus the force absorption benefit to ensure the athletes are recovered sufficiently, since this is the part of the season they train all year for. My exception to this is the sports that I only see one time a week. With them, I have to fit both strength and power into one session, so the cleans cover both of those needs. Please keep in mind that I always have the ability to adjust loads, reps, sets, and rest time based on how each individual athlete is feeling that day. I am a firm believer in giving each athlete what they need, and not using the one size fits all program.

Now, when we do cleans, do we also do heavy deadlifts that same week? No, they achieve the bilateral hip hinge pattern through the cleans. When we do cleans or hang cleans, do we also front squat during the same week? No, of course not, they're getting the front squat stimulus out of the cleans.

As I stated before, I have the setup and staff to be able to have all my athletes perform cleans. This is not necessarily the case in every weight room.

I get asked quite often to compare the clean to the weighted jump. That's an impossible task to compare. That would be like asking to compare section 1 of this book to section 2 of this book. They should be used for different goals within the same training program, not as either/or. Think about the benefits of these two exercises. The clean gives you a bilateral hip hinge pulling movement, a high velocity bilateral upper body pull, a bilateral front squat, an absorption of force, and all while requiring an athlete to use coordination to time all these movements properly. A weighted jump requires an athlete to produce force into the ground. There would be very little velocity if the load is heavy. There are no pulling movements nor squatting movement. So, to use the weighted jump as a replacement for a clean, you now also need to program reps and sets of a hip hinge pull, a high velocity upper body pull, and a bilateral squat pattern. Then you must figure out another way to create the force absorption and the coordination benefits. You would need to dedicate an entire training session to achieve all that, when instead, it could be done in a matter of a few sets of cleans.

Now that it seems like I have rained on the parade of the weighted jump, I can tell you it is actually a staple of my program. I use it differently for different sports. But generally, I use it as a unilateral movement, and not more than 15-20% of the athletes max deadlift. The only time I program bilateral weighted jumps are for a pre-game warmup for basketball. On those I usually ask them to go 20-30% of their max deadlift. And with these, as well as cleans, I never program more than 3 reps in a set. After 3 reps, power output drops significantly.

We have covered my philosophy on how and when to utilize cleans in your program. We have covered a very efficient and effective way to teach a clean progression (I have had athletes complete the entire progression successfully in 2 training sessions, while others take a little longer). We covered actual injury data, showing that weightlifting is one of the safest things you can do in sport. If you are still uncomfortable with using cleans in your program, I would highly suggest attending one of the USA Weightlifting Coach Seminars, and / or attending one of Coach Michael Cohen's in person weightlifting clinics. He travels around the US and Canada doing these, and they are free to the host! And, as I said earlier in the book, I am happy to answer general questions on clean technique or application. I just won't answer specific programming questions as it relates to another coach's athletes, since I only know my athletes and our situation well enough to comment.

Chapter 6:

Addressing Technique Faults

As we discussed earlier in the book, many technique faults can be addressed from adjusting the set up position. With that said, I'm going to take the next few pages to cover the 7 most common technique faults I see in my athletes, as well as other athletes via social media or videos that are sent to me for opinions.

However, before we get into some specific examples, let's look at one general issue that is a common contributing factor for several faults and often overlooked in the strength & conditioning universe, but well known in the Olympic weightlifting community. That issue is shoes! So many athletes go into the weight room wearing really nice running shoes or some sweet Air Max kicks. If you know me, you know I am a huge sneakerhead and really appreciate a nice pair of kicks. However, a soft sole shoe, such as a running shoe, or an Air Max does no good in the weight room where you are asked to apply force into the floor. You lose some of that force in the cushioning of the shoe. Consider a situation where you are asked to test your max vertical jump, and you are given the option of jumping off a concrete floor, or jumping from an inflated air mattress. Which option would you choose? It doesn't take a PHD in physics to know that 100% of the time you would choose the concrete floor over the air mattress. The same reasoning applies to wearing a soft sole shoe for cleans (or squats, deadlifts, etc). Look, running shoes are made for running. I've asked my athletes multiple times, "hey, would you want to wear your golf shoes to play football? No? Then why are you wearing your running shoes to lift weights?"

Now, in an ideal world, everyone would have weightlifting shoes (my favorite are the Nike

Romaleos). The advantage of a weightlifting shoe is the raised heel puts your ankle into plantarflexion, which gives more mobility at the hip, allowing for better squat mechanics. The bottom is hard, so you don't lose any force transfer. The uppers are firm, so you get stability out of the shoe as well. However, the downside is they are expensive. A good pair of lifters will run you $200+, and asking most high school or college athletes to shell out that extra cash for a shoe they wear an hour a day isn't realistic. With that said, since I "retired" from competitive weightlifting, I don't even wear lifters anymore when I lift. I just train in my Jordan 1s or 5s. Both shoes have a hard sole, so I don't lose any energy transfer, and my hip and ankle mobility is very good, so I don't need the raised heel to maintain good squat mechanics. My point isn't that lifting in J's is ideal, but more that any shoe with a hard sole will be acceptable for an athlete without any lower body mobility issues. Even if there are ankle or hip mobility issues, there are alternative work arounds discussed below.

Fault 1: The athlete catches the bar well, but the heels come off the ground during the squat portion of the clean.

Correction 1: This could be stemming from one or more of several issues. My first check would be, can the athlete perform a body weight squat sufficiently while keeping their heel in contact with the floor?

If not, then we would look at screening hip, knee, and ankle mobility, and address it from that scenario. A corrective exercise I use often in this situation is having the athlete perform squats with a 2.5Lb plate under their heels. This is a workaround for not having weightlifting shoes.

If the heel raise is coming more as an ankle inversion, I place a plastic pen under the edge of the foot that is elevating, and ask the athlete to smash that pen as they squat. Over time, that helps correct the issue.

If you know the athlete moves well, and the problem is not mobility related, then the odds are the athlete is either starting in the set up position with the bar too far in front of them, or as they go through the 2nd pull, they are kicking the bar away from them. If the bar is too far in front at the transition from 2nd pull to catch, the athlete will have to go forward to get under the bar.

Fault 2: The athlete is kicking the bar out in front of them on the second pull, causing the athlete to move forward at the catch position. This generally results in a forward lean, heels leaving the floor at the bottom of the squat, elbows pointing down at the catch, and a very ugly concentric portion of the squat.

Correction: This is one of the easier fixes. I generally will stand directly in front of the athlete at a 90 degree angle, meaning my leg and arm are a few inches from where their bar path needs to be. I queue them "go ahead and lift, but don't hit me with the bar". You'd be amazed at how much better their bar path is on the following repetitions. I have yet to get hit (knock on wood).

Fault 3: The Starfish Power Clean. You see this one ALL over social media. The athlete is attempting a heavy, usually impressive weight power clean. Everything looks good until he/she transitions from the second pull into the catch position. Suddenly, they're about to do the splits, with their feet way outside their body. Usually this video also includes several teammates and coaches jumping around screaming in the background (yes, I said it – you guys know who you are). Let's correct this fault though. Even though the athlete made the lift, and likely got several likes on social media, it was not a good lift, nor was it as productive as it was intended to be. Catching in the starfish position puts a lot of added stress on the knee and hips. Applying force to stand that load up, using a wide stance, is also targeting different muscles than those intended when prescribing a power clean, or a clean. There is also the factor that if using correct form, the athlete could lift a larger load, thus reaping more power and strength benefits.

Correction: The starfish fault is something that gets harder and harder to correct the longer the athlete does it. I know this from personal experience. From 1995 through probably 2014, I was guilty of this fault. It took so long to fix it, and if I am being totally honest, I still starfish sometimes on a heavy power clean. That is one reason I rarely ever post a video of myself doing a power clean. The earlier on it can be addressed the better. The best way I find to correct this with my athletes is by using a marker on the floor and having them lift over it, without their feet going past the sides. In our weight room at Walton, we have the school's logo, a diamond with a

W in the center, on every platform. I set the athlete up with their feet hip width apart, which for most is to the outside edges of that W. I tell them, that on the catch, their feet need to leave the edges of the W, but cannot go outside of the diamond.

Fault 4: The athlete's feet do not leave the floor at the transition of the 2nd pull into the catch. This tends to happen with newer lifters in both the clean and the power clean.

Correction: This is generally a verbal queue. Some of the more successful queues I have used for this are as follows:

"Be more aggressive with your feet and push the floor away hard!"

"It should sound like a gunshot when you finish the pull and start the squat."

"I should hear your feet hit the ground and know you did a lift even if I am facing the other way!"

A word of caution when giving these queues is that you do not want the athlete jumping or donkey kicking. The feet should leave the floor due to the force being applied into the ground. We know Newton's 3rd Law states that every action (force) has an equal and opposite reaction. So, if an athlete applies maximal force into the ground, there has to be an equal and opposite reaction. The natural reaction would be that at the peak, the athlete leaves contact with the floor. By keeping the feet on the floor, that athlete is basically hitting the breaks on their velocity. However, we know speed under the bar is important to make the lift successful. So the athlete MUST return to ground contact as quickly and aggressively as possible. That is where the load "foot stomp" noise is made, not by actually stomping or jumping. With that said, I would much rather have to address a stomper than someone not leaving the ground. If they're stomping, we know they're using maximal force, but they're just going to lose speed under the bar. And if the goal is power production, I am happy to make that trade while I work over time to address the jumping/stomping fault. I do this by queuing the athlete to return to the ground as quickly as possible.

Fault 5: Catching the bar low or with elbows pointing down.

Correction: This one is a little trickier. I have several ways of addressing this fault, but it really comes down to knowing the athlete and understanding the biomechanics of their sport.

If I know the athlete is intelligent, moves well, and plays a throwing sport, such as baseball, softball, or lacrosse, I simply start by explaining the danger to their UCL by catching low or catching with the elbows down. Again, this is for a smart athlete, who does not have mobility issues in the shoulders, wrists, or elbows. You'd be surprised at how quickly they adjust when understanding it puts strain on the elbow.

Now, in a scenario where it is a younger athlete, or one who is not as strong, or not a throwing athlete, but are who has no mobility issues, I address it completely differently. I use two exercises to address this. First, I set them in a squat rack, with the bar set up for a clean finish. I then ask that they stand the bar up without using their hands. Yes, I get some strange looks. But I let them figure it out, and they soon realize they need to use their shoulders as a shelf to stand the bar up. I then explain, that is where the barbell needs to be when you catch the clean. From there, we run through some clean finishes, working on driving the elbows under the bar at the bottom. The clean finish is explained in the definitions portion of Section 3.

Fault 6: Catching the bar with elbows down and a closed grip.

Correction: This can be addressed in two ways. The first thing I generally try is simply to explain to the athlete that they only need a finger or two on the bar at the catch position. This works since in sport performance training setting, we are not doing a clean and jerk. If you were training a competitive weightlifter, this might not be the ideal approach since they would need to re-adjust the hand placement to be able to go into the jerk.

If the simple verbal queue doesn't fix the issue, then setting them up for a front squat, in a rack, and asking them to just hold the bar in the fingertips while performing a front squat generally works.

Fault 7: Hips staying muted.

Correction: This one is trickier. You first need to find out why the athlete isn't extending the hips. It could be related to the set up – if the bar is too far in front of their shins, the timing will be off on the pull. The same result would apply if the athlete's knees are too far in front of the bar at the setup, or if their torso is angled too far forward. Many times this can be fixed by queuing the athlete to raise their chest in the setup position.

Another way I have addressed this is to put chalk on the bar and ask the athlete to make sure the bar leaves a chalk mark on their upper quads as it brushes against the leg on the pull. An alternative way I have explained it to more advanced athletes is that the hip pattern for the pull needs to be similar to that of a kettlebell swing.

If it is not setup related, it could just be a timing issue. If this is the case, I generally have the athlete work out of the hang position to create a neurological pattern (muscle memory), so they get used to transitioning into the second pull from the proper position, with the hips extended.

Section 3

Definitions

When training athletes, consistent vocabulary is vital. While as coaches, we know multiple names for practically every movement, interchanging terms can be confusing to an athlete. Therefore, I want to provide the standard terms I use, and what I use them for. Obviously, this is not a complete list, but instead it highlights the most commonly confused terms I see from social media, coaching conferences, and athlete discussions. These definitions are not in alphabetical order, instead, I listed them in the order I find most beneficial in teaching the terminology to an athlete.

Clean: Taking the load from the floor to the shoulders by way of squatting under said load, in order to catch the weight at the lowest point possible. Doing this efficiently maintains the load traveling in an upwards direction, thus not changing the momentum and allowing a larger weight to be lifted. You get the squatting benefit out of this movement. Generally, I program this for off-season training.

Power Clean: Taking the load from the floor to the shoulders without dropping into a full squat (below parallel). Less weight can be lifted with this variation, but it is possible for some athletes to generate more power this way. Additionally, it is less stressful on the legs, and I generally program this during the season for some sports.

Hang Clean: This movement starts by deadlifting the weight off the floor, standing up to full hip extension, and maintaining full elbow extension. You then drive the hips backwards lowering the bar to a point somewhere between the hips and knees before changing direction to initiate the weight traveling away from the ground at a high velocity. You then squat under the bar (below parallel) to follow the pattern of the **Clean**. I generally incorporate this in the pre-season for most sports, and in season for the sports I see less than 3 days a week. It also helps save stress from the Central nervous system over multiple reps, since each subsequent rep in the set begins from the hips, without returning the bar to the ground (avoiding the deadlift/first pull portion of the clean).

Hang Power Clean: This is the combination of the **Clean** and the **Hang Clean.** This is the LEAST taxing variation of a clean, and I primarily use it for in-season athletes I see 3 or more days per week.

High Hang Position: Barbell at the hips, hips fully extended, elbows fully extended.

Low Hang Position: Barbell at the Knees, hips slightly flexed, hamstrings fully loaded, elbows completely extended.

1st Pull: The Liftoff (Deadlift portion) of the **Clean.**

2nd Pull: The portion of the **Clean** after achieving full hip extension, and from the start of elbow flexion.

Clean Pull: The combination of the **1st Pull** and **2nd Pull**. In the sport of weightlifting, this is done generally AFTER performing all clean repetitions, and uses a load greater than 100% of the athletes 1 Rep Max Clean. The goal is to adapt to pulling a heavier weight off the ground. However, the Clean Pull has found its way into the strength & conditioning world as an alternative to performing an actual **Clean**, with the concept of benefiting from the velocity portion of the power equation.

Catch: This is the portion of the **Clean** or **Power Clean** or any hanging variation where the athlete receives the load on the shoulders.

Front Rack: This is the position of holding the load on the shoulders, elbows fully flexed and pointing forward, humerus of each arm parallel to each other and parallel to the floor. A great coaching queue I use with this is the elbows are your headlights. The barbell needs to be resting on the shoulders. If the athlete is unable to perform this, they must first improve wrist mobility before attempting to **catch** a load.

Tall Clean: Starting holding the barbell at the hips, while standing in full plantar flexion, elbows extended, and shoulders shrugged. From that position, the athlete "drops" under the bar catching it in the bottom of a front squat.

Clean Finish: As described in Section 2, the bar sits on top of jerk boxes, or in a squat rack, or in the safety spotter straps/bars, at a height where you can hold the bar at the position of the top of the first pull. You then squat under the bar, keeping your chest next to the bar as you descend. You shoot your elbows under the bar, now at the low point of your squat, while in the front rack position. Then you stand up. It is imperative to start with the bar in a rack or on boxes and NOT lift the bar off that platform until you stand up out of the bottom of the squat. Otherwise, you would be performing a **Tall Clean,** not a Clean Finish.

Photo by Cesar Morales @ LIFTINGLIFE

My son Lee back stage with me in Miami for the USAW
American Open Series

Here is a picture of the platforms and rack set up we have
at Walton. You can see the safety straps in the racks that I
use to teach the Clean Finish. I also want to point out,
how we have defined lifting areas on the floor. I know
some weight rooms do not have this. However, for liability
reasons, I strongly recommend having a defined space for
each athlete when doing any variation of the Olympic lifts.

This was our old weight room at Walton. While we didn't have the floor marked off the same way as the new room, we did have stall mats representing the designated lifting areas. Again, this is for both athlete safety as well as liability.

Thank you for taking the time to read my book. I really hope you were able to get some beneficial information from how I teach and utilize the clean with my athletes. I truly believe as Strength & Conditioning / Sport Performance Coaches we have a great community and can learn different ways of teaching movement from each other. Please feel free to reach out to me on social media with any questions or clarifications you may want. The goal of writing this book was to help share the knowledge!

Twitter & Instagram: @CoachCris_

Linkedin: CoachChrisRomano

In strength,

Appendix:

1. Drechsler, "USAW Sports Performance Coach Course" USA Weightlifting 2013

2. Hamil, B. "Relative safety of weightlifting and weight training" Journal of Strength & Conditioning Research. 8(1):53-57. 1994

Made in the USA
Monee, IL
24 May 2021